PESCADERO

A CALIFORNIA COASTAL TOWN

Phyllis L. Neumann

This book is dedicated to the wonderful people of Pescadero.

I would like to give my appreciation to Meredith Reynolds and Greg Timm for reviewing the book for accuracy and, most of all, to Bob, my husband, and Janet Cook, my granddaughter, for their ongoing advice and support throughout this process.

Pescadero Photography
a subsidiary of Penngrove Publications

P.O. Box 798, Pescadero, CA 94060
(650) 879-0769 • phyllneum@aol.com
www.pescaderophotography.com

Contents

History of Pescadero

Only an hour's drive south from San Francisco on Highway 1 lies the tiny town of Pescadero. This quaint town still retains a good deal of its 19th century charm with many historic buildings still remaining. By world standards, however, Pescadero is a very new community, inhabited by the Ohlone Indians until the early 1800s.

The Ohlone Indians. For thousands of years the Ohlones made their homes in the coastal regions, from Big Sur to San Francisco. They set up about 40 small villages, or "tribelets," with approximately 100-250 Ohlones living in each village. Each tribelet had its own territory, name, language and chief. The region surrounding Pescadero was home to three villages: one in the Pescadero area, one at Año Nuevo, and the largest one at White House Flat, south of Pigeon Point.

Europeans began arriving in the area around 1769, eventually building seven missions in Ohlone territory. Their arrival greatly affected the Ohlone population by spreading disease and starvation, increasing infant mortality and dramatically changing the Ohlone's way of life. Sadly, only a handful of Ohlones survived into the 20th century.

The Mexican Period. Mexico won its independence from Spain in 1821, and Pescadero became part of Mexico. The Mexican government granted eight ranchos along the San Mateo coast. In 1833 Juan Jose Gonzàles petitioned for and was granted the land called Rancho El Pescadero. There he built a small adobe on Pescadero Creek where he grazed his cattle. This became the major economic activity in the area.

When the Mexican-American War ended in 1848 Pescadero became part of the United States. At that time Pescadero was just a tiny Mexican village with one rancho and about 500 cattle. A few remaining Ohlones were also scattered in the area. After Gonzàles died, his widow was forced to sell off his land in order to pay the legal fees and past debts. The balance of the land was sold in a probate auction in 1856 to James Brennen, a San Francisco attorney and financial investor who envisioned much promise for Pescadero.

The Town. Pescadero (Spanish for "fishing place") was not established until 1856. At that time the area was a farming and ranching community. Farmers, dairymen, ranchers and lumbermen, generally moving from New England, built their homes according to familiar east coast architecture. This is reflected today in many of the original homes of Pescadero.

By the 1890s Pescadero had become a popular seaside resort with a bustling population of about 500 residents. Surprisingly, it was the fourth largest town in San Mateo County. Stage Road was the main highway tying Pescadero to San Francisco. The business district developed around the intersection of Stage Road and Pescadero Creek Road. There was a store, post office and school; saloons and churches were built shortly after. The Swanton House and the Pescadero Hotel were booked for reservations months in advance.

Ocean Shore Railway. Tourists came to Pescadero by stage coach from as far away as San Francisco, Santa Cruz and beyond, but it was a long and difficult journey. In 1905, in order to attract vacationers and tourists, the Ocean Shore Railway Company began construction of a high-speed electric railway that ran from San Francisco to Tunitas Glen in the north, and from Santa Cruz to Swanton in the south. However, the 26-mile middle leg of the line between Tunitas Glen and Swanton was never completed. Tourists coming to Pescadero by train were dropped off at Tunitas Glen where they would be met by carriages and wagons, and eventually by a Stanley Steamer. The 1906 earthquake disrupted construction of the railroad before the gap that included Pescadero could be built.

Attractions. Pescadero had much to offer vacationers in those days. They enjoyed fishing for steelhead trout in Pescadero Creek and for salmon in the Pacific Ocean. Sportsmen hunted for fowl, deer and even grizzly bear in Pescadero Marsh (now a wildlife refuge). Others enjoyed the majestic redwood forests and the pristine beaches. They picked berries and wildflowers, and watched for whales from various vantage points along the coast. Gem-collecting at Pebble Beach was also a popular pastime, where beautiful colorful stones could be found — including jade, opals, agate and carnelians. Most of all, tourists enjoyed the cool summers when areas farther inland were sweltering.

DOWNTOWN PESCADERO IN 1913

COURTESY OF THE PESCADERO HISTORICAL SOCIETY

Pescadero Today

Pescadero remains a small diverse community, still retaining a good deal of its 19th century charm, with as many as fourteen historic buildings remaining essentially unchanged in structure. Once the Cabrillo Highway (Hwy 1) was built, by-passing Pescadero, the town lost its popularity as a resort town. The Peninsula Open Space Trust purchased many acres, preserving the small-town atmosphere. Unfortunately, increased housing costs forced many residents to leave the area.

Pescadero is a close-knit community where everyone seems to know everyone, and residents casually stop their cars in the middle of the street to talk to their friends and neighbors. The flag at the post office is traditionally flown at half-mast should a resident of Pescadero pass away. There are around 100 residences and businesses in town and its surrounding area, with approximately 800 registered voters. Agriculture is still Pescadero's main economic resource.

Pescadero enjoys a moderate climate throughout the year, with relatively little temperature variation due to the moderate influence of the ocean. Temperatures range between 43°F. to 68°F. Summers are warm and dry, with the warmest months between August and October. Winters are cool and wet, with an average annual precipitation between 20 to 25 inches. Approximately 80 percent of rainfall occurs between November and March. Pescadero and Butano Creeks, which flow year-round, meander through town. During heavy winter storms they occasionally overflow their banks, flooding Pescadero Creek Road and blocking the main access into town.

DOWNTOWN PESCADERO FACING NORTH

Pescadero is still a popular weekend tourist destination throughout the year, especially during the summer months, because of the local beaches, old redwood groves and hiking trails. There are several interesting boutiques to visit along Stage Road, Pescadero's main street, and berry-picking at Phipp's Ranch is a popular pastime. Pescadero Creek is still a salmon-spawning stream and cattle still graze on the hills. The Pescadero Marsh Natural Preserve, at the intersection of Highway 1 and Pescadero Creek Road, is now protected by the California Coastal Act and is a popular destination for bird watching. Cabrillo Highway (Hwy 1), two miles west of Pescadero, is still considered one of the most beautiful stretches of road in the United States.

One of Pescadero's main attractions is Duarte's Tavern, where waiting for a table on weekends can sometimes take up to an hour. The Pescadero Country Store hosts weekend barbecues, and Norm's Market bakes delicious bread and makes up great sandwiches. Los Amigos Tacqueria, housed in the corner gas station, serves authentic Mexican food. On the third Sunday of the month the Pescadero Community Church hosts a pancake breakfast and, on the third weekend in August, the annual Pescadero Art and Fun Faire (PAFF) is held at the I.D.E.S. Hall.

On July 2, 2006 Pescadero celebrated its 150th anniversary. The Pescadero Historical Society set up a mini-museum at the Native Sons Hall with displays of historic photographs, antique furnishings, photo albums, oral histories and updated maps for the self-guided *Pescadero Walking Tour*. The I.D.E.S. Hall hosted a free barbecue and pot luck for Pescadero residents complete with live music and, in the afternoon, a new town photo was taken. The whole town came out to help Pescadero celebrate its special day in style.

DOWNTOWN PESCADERO FACING SOUTH

Stage Road South

Until around 1919, the south end of Stage Road, from Pescadero Road south to the end, was originally called Turkey Lane.

Native Sons Hall
112 Stage Road

The Native Sons Community Hall was built in 1889 and dedicated in 1990 as a Methodist-Episcopal church, one of three churches in Pescadero. Due to dwindling membership the building was eventually abandoned in 1915. After that the building went through several changes. In 1920 it was converted into a community center, then it became a town library, a movie theater and a health center. In 1928 the building was used as a Japanese Cultural Center and language school by the Japanese-American community living in Pescadero. This ended after the attack on Pearl Harbor in 1942.

Today the building is co-owned by the Native Sons of the Golden West and the Pescadero Historical Society and is used for community functions throughout the year. The building is currently being restored by the Pescadero History Project.

I.O.O.F. Hall
110 Stage Road

In 1874, a chapter of the International Order of Odd Fellows (I.O.O.F.) was organized in Pescadero, which soon became one of the most active fraternal groups in the area. In 1878, the Order bought this property in order to build a meeting hall for the group. The building was made more elaborate in 1890 with the addition of an overhang, decorative brackets were added under the eaves and a veranda with a balcony was built.

The Hall saw a good deal of activity. Town and committee meetings were held, and dinners and dances were regular events. Remodeling destroyed the original classic lines of the building. The house is currently owned by Tom and Shirley Hickson.

William Knapp House
80 Stage Road

This house was originally owned and probably built by William Knapp around 1863, and is one of the oldest houses in the community. Designed along vaguely classical lines in Greek Revival style, the house is similar in design and materials to the Alexander Moore house, built in 1853, which was located where the Phipps Ranch now stands. Knapp lived in the house with his wife, Julia, and their several children. One of the daughters, May, married Edmond Moore, who was one of the last stagecoach drivers in the area. They continued to live in the home after Julia died. The house was lived in by a member of the Knapp family from 1863 until 1966.

Like other structures south of Pescadero Road, the house was spared by the fires of the 1920s that took most of the Pescadero business district. The house is currently owned by Ann and Greg Timm.

I.D.E.S. Hall and Chapel

Stage Road
(650) 879-0848

I.D.E.S. (Irmandade do Divino Espirito Santo), or Brotherhood of the Holy Spirit, is a Portuguese fraternal order. The largest of the three buildings on this property is a one-story structure, which was built around 1914. It had horizontal wood ship-lap siding and a gabled roof. The chapel, the smallest building, was shown in an 1878 lithograph.

I.D.E.S. CHAPEL

Community events are held in all three buildings throughout the year: the Easter Celebration in March, the Chamarita Festival in May, the Pescadero Arts and Fun Festival (PAFF) in August, the Christmas Bazaar in December, along with the popular Crab, Wild Game and Cioppino Feeds.

Downtown Pescadero

Los Amigos Tacqueria & Market
1999 Pescadero Road
(650) 879-0232

This corner was once the site of the famous Swanton House, a grand hotel built in the late 1800s. Around 1926 the hotel and its six guest cottages burned to the ground. All that remains of that grand hotel is an old magnolia tree enclosed by a chainlink fence.

That corner has now become the site of the only gas station and Mexican restaurant in Pescadero. With only a small sign displayed on the side of the building, Los Amigos is always busy serving authentic Mexican food to eat in or take-out. The restaurant was written up in the *New York Times* on July 21, 2006 as having "the best tacos this side of Mexico." The mini-market offers a wide range of goods, as well as fresh-baked Mexican bread and pastries. The restaurant is open daily, from 10 a.m. to 10 p.m.; the mini-market and gas station are open daily, from 6 a.m. to 10 p.m.

Pescadero Thrift Shop

2041 Pescadero Road
(650) 879-9613

The Pescadero Thrift Shop has been owned and operated by South Coast Children's Services since 1988, and is one of the organization's major sources of financial support for funding youth programs and activities. People come from all over the Bay Area to buy affordable clothing, household items, jewelry, books, toys, and furniture when it is available. Open Wednesday through Sunday, 11:00 a.m. to 5:30 p.m.; closed Monday and Tuesday.

Duarte's Tavern

202 Stage Road
(650) 879-0464 • www.duartestavern.com

Duarte's (pronounced DOO-arts) was started in 1894 by Frank Duarte and is considered to be a Pescadero landmark, serving an average of 13,000 people per month. Waiting for a table on weekends can sometimes take up to an hour. Though fire destroyed the building in the 1920s, the original bar was saved.

Still a family-run operation, Ron and Lynn Duarte entered the business in the 1950s, and today fourth-generation Tim and his sister, Kathy, also play an active role. Duarte's has grown from two employees in the '50s to over sixty-five employees today. Back in the '30s, the restaurant mainly served sandwiches and ice cream. Today there is an extensive menu, featuring Duarte's famous artichoke soup, equally famous crab cioppino, fresh fish and a wine list of over two hundred different labels. The restaurant also grows its own fresh vegetables and stays in close contact with local fishermen, thus assuring fresh fish and vegetables every day. Open daily 7 a.m. to 9 p.m.

Made in Pescadero
216 Stage Road
(650) 879-9128 • www.madeinpescadero.com

Made in Pescadero is a working gallery, displaying the very finest hand-crafted furniture, art and accessories by the area's most talented craftsmen and artists. Nowhere else will you find this personally-chosen collection of custom furniture, paintings, pottery and jewelry. The store is owned and operated by Ken Periat. Open Monday and Friday 12:00 p.m. to 4:00 p.m., Saturday and Sunday 11:00 a.m. to 6:00 p.m.

Stage Road Shops
248 Stage Road
(650) 879-0476

In the late 1890s this building housed a livery stable and blacksmith shop. The building was set back from the street to accommodate horse-drawn carriages and coaches which could pull right up to the building to be shod. Over the years it was used as a stable, a storage area and an art studio.

Today the building houses a lovely boutique which sells gemstones, silver jewelry, antique reproductions in cast iron, vases, china, scented candles scented, coastal lavender and body care products, stained glass garden lighting, linens, kitchen collectibles and clothing. The store is owned and operated by Judy Periat. Open Friday through Sunday, 11 a.m. to 6 p.m.

Pescadero Creekside Barn

248 Stage Road
(650) 879-0868 • www.pescaderolodging.com

The upstairs loft of Stage Road Shops is the Pescadero Creekside Barn, a unique and cozy overnight lodging for two. The Barn features kitchen facilities, a queen-size brass bed, an antique clawfoot tub, a Dutch-style loft door overlooking Stage Road and a private courtyard. You can also enjoy the modern amenities of a gas fireplace, stereo, television, VCR/DVD and telephone. The Barn is owned and operated by Rob and Cotton Skinner.

Luna Sea
250 Stage Road
(650) 879-1207

This 100-year-old redwood-framed house was originally the childhood home of Gordon Moore, co-founder of Intel, one of Silicon Valley's largest and most successful companies. Walter Moore, Gordon's father, served as Town Constable for four consecutive terms, or 16 years, and was a respected member of the community.

Today Luna Sea is a lovely boutique, garden and gallery that features unique handcrafted gift items such as jewelry, artwork, outdoor sculptures, ceramic garden torches, bath products, stained glass and clothes. The store is owned and operated by Janice Keen. Open Friday through Sunday, 11:00 a.m. to 6:00 p.m., Monday, 12:00 p.m. to 5:00 p.m.

First National Bank
239 Stage Road
(650) 879-0785 • www.fnbnorcal.com

A. P. Giannini's Bank of Italy first opened its doors in 1927, and the small stuccoed building with its tall arched windows and flat roof has been a fixture in Pescadero ever since. The bank was changed to Bank of America, but closed in the summer of 1997 due to corporate restructuring. The First National Bank of Northern California opened shortly after, offering continued service to its residents.

The bank still retains its old-fashioned flavor in that residents are known by name and there's seldom a line. There is an ATM window that is available for quick cash. The bank is open Monday through Thursday 9 a.m. to 4 p.m., Friday 9 a.m. to 6 p.m.

Pescadero Country Store
251 Stage Road
(650) 879-0410

Formerly Muzzi's Market & Deli, the store was originally owned and run by the Williamson family. In 1869 J. C. Williamson came to Pescadero and, after working for different merchants, opened his own store in 1885. Over the years the Williamsons had three stores which all burned down. Around 1998 the Muzzi family purchased the market, and it was since bought by Cindy Simms. The famous stagecoach mural above the door was originally painted by Al Krebs and recently renovated by Debbie Bennett.

The deli features delicious sandwiches served on fresh-baked bread, as well as a full line of specialty coffees. The market is well stocked with everything from fresh produce to camping and beach supplies, as well as homemade sweets and desserts. On weekends, when the weather is nice, the store offers an outdoor barbecue, including ribs, tri-tip sandwiches and live music. Fresh-made pizza is planned to open shortly. Open Monday through Saturday 9 a.m. to 6 p.m., Sunday 10 a.m. to 5 p.m.

Arcangeli Grocery Company/Norm's Market

287 Stage Road
(650) 879-0147 • www.normsmarket.com

Norm's Market was originally started in 1929 by Norm Benedetti's maternal grandfather, Sante Arcangeli. It was called Pescadero Bakery and Grocery and was located across the street. Now in larger quarters, the store is run by Norm Benedetti and his two sons, Mike and Don.

The aroma of warm, freshly baked bread greets you at the door. Norm's is stocked with groceries and locally grown produce, and specializes in its Italian artichoke, French garlic-herb and sourdough breads. The store is now offering a new line of gourmet salsas, sauces, spreads, appetizers and marinades. The store also boasts a large selection of wine, gourmet coffee and over 70 varieties of cheese. The butcher shop in the rear sells homemade pork sausage, linguica and chorizo, picnic foods and made-to-order sandwiches. Open daily 10 a.m. to 6 p.m.

Country Roads Antiques
290 Stage Road
(650) 897-0452

Once a blacksmith shop, this charming old building now holds a great variety of antiques and collectibles, such as old furniture, paintings and nick-nacks, a bird cage and an old chest brimming over with linen. Owned and operated by Rob and Cotton Skinner. Open weekends, 12:00 to 5:00 p.m.

James McCormick House

358 Stage Road
(650) 521-2628 • www.mccormickhousepescadero.com

On the north end of downtown, across from the Pescadero Church, almost hidden by trees, is the James McCormick House. Built in the late 1860s and influenced by the Classical Revival, it is considered to be one of the most sophisticated of the houses built in this era, and also almost the mirror image of the William Knapp House at the other end of town.

James was born in Ireland and emigrated to New York in 1848. A very enterprising young man, James moved to Pescadero in 1864 and did some farming as well as buying several businesses. The McCormick & Son's store housed the telephone office and a library. James then acquired large timber holdings in the Butano area and began a career in lumbering. James' son, James Jr., became a master carpenter, and built many homes in Pescadero.

The McCormick House is now used as a "Bed and Biscuit" Inn and is currently owned and run by Lisa Tune and Mauro Torriggiani.

Pescadero Community Church
363 Stage Road

Built in 1867, the Pescadero Community Church is the oldest surviving Protestant church on the San Francisco Peninsula still on its original foundation. The simple redwood frame building, with its square louvered bell tower at the entry, is built in the classical revival style and reflects the New England background of many of Pescadero's settlers. The bell tower was added in 1890. In 1984 the church became California Registered Historical Landmark No. 949.

Today the church is used as a town meeting place as well as a social and spiritual center. Its monthly Sunday pancake breakfasts have been a popular event with the locals for years. The church serves Pescadero, not only as a link to the past, but as an integral part of present-day community life.

Pescadero Creek Inn
393 Stage Road
(888) 307-1898 • www.pescaderocreekinn.com

This 100-year-old farmhouse was originally built around 1898. It was converted to a three-unit apartment house in 1933 and the cottage was added out back. The building was condemned in 1987. It was then purchased in 1991 by Ken and Penny Donnelly, who completely renovated it in 1993 and made it into a bed-and-breakfast.

The Pescadero Creek Inn offers a tranquil country setting, a place to relax in front of a beautiful stone fireplace or a lovely garden by the banks of Pescadero Creek. Decorated with period antiques, each room has a queen-sized down featherbed and a private bath with antique a claw-foot tub. A delicious gourmet breakfast is included, which is made from organic produce and eggs from local farms.

Stage Road North

Mt. Hope / St. Anthony's Cemetery
About ¼-mile north of town on Stage Road

On a hill overlooking the road leading to Pescadero, you will find this historic cemetery, which is now divided into two two-acre parcels. The southern part of the cemetery is owned by the Pescadero Community Church and the northern part, which was purchased from Bartlett V. Weeks in 1875, is owned by St. Anthony's Catholic Church. Burials began in the cemetery in the 1860s.

Today, processions of mourners still follow the coffins from either the Pescadero Community Church or St. Anthony's Catholic Church, and follow Stage Road up the hill to where the recently deceased are laid to rest alongside of Pescadero's 19th-century pioneers.

Heading North along Stage Road

If you follow Stage Road north from downtown Pescadero, past the Mt. Hope/St. Anthony's Cemetery, you will travel along this peaceful, picturesque road lined with large eucalyptus trees and dotted with occasional white-fenced farms with horses and sheep grazing in the fields.

North Street

Old Blacksmith Shop
860 North Street

John Goulson was born in Lincolnshire, England, on the estate of the Duke of Rutland. His family had been blacksmiths for over 200 years. In the 1840s, Goulson and his family emigrated to Wisconsin, arriving in Pescadero in 1866, where he opened his own blacksmith shop. His son, Alfred, continued to run the shop after his father's death. The property, which is owned by John Dixon, has been kept with the original sign on the front of the old building.

The Tower
785 North Street (650) 879-0841 • www.thetowerpescadero.com

This newly built house is fashioned after the old water towers which can be found in many of the backyards in Pescadero. Overnight lodging includes all the comforts of home, including a full kitchen, king-size bed, and a large living and dining area. Modern amenities include satellite TV, Internet service, telephone and a 360° view of the coastal hills.

St. Anthony's Church
696 North Street

Construction of this small Roman Catholic Church began in 1867, and its tower was added in 1888. The building retains the architecture of the community and is similar in design to the Pescadero Community Church.

Though Classical Revival in style, the spire shows a strong Gothic influence. Although the town of Pescadero remained relatively untouched by the 1906 earthquake, it shook the small church off its foundation, which was then set back on its base and repaired.

Pescadero Union High School
429 North Street

The Pescadero Union High School was dedicated on November 29, 1925, with 37 students enrolled. This building, along with Norm's Market, are the only two examples of Spanish Revival style in Pescadero. In 1960 a new high school was built off Cloverdale Road. It serves both Pescadero and La Honda from ninth through twelfth grades, and has an average enrollment of 130 students. The old high school building is now used for housing migrant farm workers.

Harley Farms Goat Dairy
205 North Street (650) 879-0480 • www.harleyfarms.com

Dee Harley, who was born in Yorkshire, England, started Harley Farms in 1989 with just six goats. She rebuilt a 1910 nine-acre cow dairy farm, which now houses the cheese-making room and milking parlor. There are over 220 American Alpine goats, producing a batch of new kids each spring.

The artisan goat cheese has received the American Cheese Society Award for five consecutive years and, in March 2007, Dee was given the "Farmer of the Year" award. These delicious award-winning cheeses are usually decorated with a variety of fruits, herbs, and edible flowers, all grown in the garden.

Two-hour group tours are available on Saturdays at 1 p.m., offering a behind-the-scenes look at this award-winning goat dairy farm. The Cheese Shop is open weekends 11 a.m. to 5 p.m.

Goulson Street

Goulson Street, the small street perpendicular to North Street, was originally the main street of Pescadero with the Post Office on the corner. The street led to a bridge across the creek that joined Pescadero Creek Road.

Bartlett V. Weeks House
172 Goulson Street

Bartlett V. Weeks moved to Pescadero in 1858 from Kennebec County, Maine. He purchased 157 acres from Juan Jose Gonzàles and moved with his family into the old Gonzales home north of Pescadero Creek. Weeks built a wooden-frame house in 1872 on what is now called Goulson Street.

Although the original date of the house is still in dispute, it was thought to be built as early as 1872, or even earlier. The fan-like ornamentation on the front porch was added later, as well as additions to the back and sides. The house sits diagonally on its lot, having a true north-south orientation; Goulson Street, which was built later, does not.

The house today is virtually unchanged from its original structure, and is currently owned and occupied by Ed Weeks, Bartlett Weeks' grandson. Marie, Ed's beloved wife, recently passed away. The house, always well-maintained and landscaped, makes it one of the most attractive houses in town.

Pescadero Road

Pescadero Sign
Intersection of Highway 1 and Pescadero Road

Two miles east of Highway 1 lies the historic town of Pescadero. Back in the late 1800s Pescadero was a popular resort town with hotels, saloons, restaurants, shops and a bustling population of about 500 residents. Today Pescadero remains a small diverse community, still retaining a good deal of its 19th century charm. Pescadero and its surrounding area house around 100 residences and businesses, with approximately 800 registered voters. Many historic buildings remain essentially unchanged, and agriculture is still Pescadero's main economic resource. Pescadero Creek, which flows year-round, still spawn steelhead salmon. Facing north across Pescadero Road lies Pescadero March Natural Preserve, a wildlife refuge for more than 150 species of birds as well as kites, deer, raccoons, foxes and skunks.

Looking Down Pescadero Road

This panorama was taken from the hill on Bean Hollow Road, just off Pescadero Road. It overlooks Pescadero Road, the main road to Pescadero. If you follow the homes leading to Pescadero you can just make out the large barn with the letters "Level Lea Farm" painted on the roof. Just across the road, standing alone in the plowed field, is the white Chandler house and barn. The flagpole stands at the intersection of Pescadero and Stage Roads. Turning south (right) on Stage Road you can see the Pescadero Post Office and the homes lining the road. Turning north (left) at the flag pole is downtown Pescadero. The large pink

building is Duarte's Tavern, and to the right of that is the two-story Pescadero Thrift Shop. Heading north along Stage Road, nestled in the trees, you can make out the steeple of the Pescadero Community Church.

The farmland along Pescadero Road is owned by Level Lea Farm. Artichokes, Brussels sprouts, fava beans and pumpkins are planted and harvested in these fields and sold locally throughout the area. After the fall harvest, the fields are usually left fallow during the winter months when the fields can often flood from heavy storms.

Chandler House and Barn
1740 Pescadero Road

This vernacular farmhouse with the barn behind it was built in the late 1850s, making it one of the oldest existing structures in the community. The large sequoia in front of the barn is over 100 years old. Lafayette Chandler, who came to Pescadero from Bangor, Maine, bought the farm in 1860, which originally consisted of three rooms. The house was sold in 1879 to James Moore, whose brother, Alexander Moore, built the barn behind the house. Layers of Portuguese, Japanese, Danish and Italian newspapers were tacked on the walls of the attic to act as insulation, telling the history of the people of Pescadero. The house was reacquired by Lafayette's daughter, Sylvia "Elma" Chandler Weeks in 1919 and recently restored by the family. The house still remains in the family today. Chandler Burnside Sawyer was born in February 1996, and lives there with her father, Ed. The property is currently owned by Jim and Meredith Reynolds.

Chandler Barn (Level Lea Farm)
1759 Pescadero Road

The 140 year-old barn, owned by Jim and Meredith Reynolds, has been in Meredith's family since before the Civil War. Four Weeks brothers moved from Maine, along with Meredith's great, great, great uncle, Lafayette Chandler, who bought the property in 1860. Jim and Meredith have lived on the land since the late 1970s in a house built in 1914 by Asa Weeks, one of Meredith's ancestors. The name "Level Lea," meaning newly cleared, level pastureland, consists of 192 acres, and is the last remaining unprotected land between Pescadero and the ocean.

The barn used to be the home of Artichoke Joe, who sold fresh artichokes, strawberries, peas, Brussels sprouts, fava beans and pumpkins which were grown on the farmland just across Pescadero Road. Now it is a working barn and the home of Stable Solutions (www.astablesolution.com), a manufacturer of fragrant handmade soap, which is owned and operated by Monique Hodgkinson.

Phipps Country Store and Farm

2700 Pescadero Road
(650) 879-0787 • www.phippscountry.com

Located one mile east of town on Pescadero Road is Phipps Country Store. It began in 1978 as an old garage with a dirt floor, a picnic table for the countertop, and a cigar box for the cash register. The store was opened by several of the Phipps children to learn the business of selling produce from the farm, and to keep them occupied during the summer months.

Today Phipps Ranch is still a family-owned operation. There is a fresh produce area, a room with bins of unusual homegrown beans, walls filled with fresh herbs and spices, a plant nursery, and beautiful herb and flower gardens spread all around the store. Beyond the store is a barnyard where farm animals and all kinds of birds live year-round. From May through September you can pick strawberries, and in June you can pick olallieberries. Open April through October, 10:00 a.m. to 6:00 p.m.; November through March, 10:00 a.m. to 5:00 p.m.

Pescadero Beaches

Pescadero State Beach
Intersection of Highway 1 and Pescadero Creek Road

Pescadero State Beach has a mile-long shoreline with sandy beach coves, rocky cliffs, tide pools, fishing spots and picnic facilities. The headlands are at the northern end of a great block of Cretaceous-age rocks that crop out along the coast. The off-shore rocks, called "sea stacks," are a haven for bird life and other marine wildlife. During the winter pebbles accumulate on the beach during high seas, usually from winter storms. During the calmer summer months sand accumulates on the beach.

Pebble Beach
2½ miles south of Pescadero on Highway 1

Pebble Beach is a small beach cove where pebbles and sand continuously accumulate and vanish. It is named after the many polished fragments of agates, opals, jaspers and carnelians found on the beach. Heavy winter storms also erode the large sandstone rocks, creating a honeycomb-like surface called "tafoni."

This small beach has been a favorite gathering place for visitors since the 1860s. Each morning the Swanton House in Pescadero would transport their guests to the beach by wagon to enjoy the sun and to collect pebbles.

In contrast to the north side, the south side of Pebble Beach has an entirely different setting. Waves crash dramatically over the rocks, leaving a series of miniature waterfalls and frothy tide pools.

ERODED HONEYCOMB EFFECT IN THE SHAPE OF A DRAGONFLY

ROCK FORMATIONS IN THE SHAPE OF ELEPHANT SEALS

Gazos Beach
10 miles south of Pescadero on Highway 1

Just south of the Pigeon Point Lighthouse lies Gazos Beach, a lovely arc of beach that lies nestled off Highway 1. The beach is protected from the wind by sand dunes that are covered in head-high vegetation. Gazos Beach offers a lovely view of California's most beautiful stretch of coast. An estuary is located nearby, which is perfect for avid bird watchers. This area is easily affected by wind and other conditions and is best viewed on nice sunny days when there is little or no wind. Weather can also be unpredictable here, so layered clothing is recommended. The beach is open from 8 a.m. to sunset; no beach fires are permitted or removal of shells, driftwood and other natural beach features.

Gazos Creek traverses many miles in its course from the mountains before emptying out into the sea through Gazos Beach. It cuts through rock, transporting materials, nurturing plants and creating habitat. The creek is rich in varied and diverse habitats and is a protected steelhead salmon spawning ground. Marbled murrelets, small sea birds, nest on nearby ridges. A rough trail runs along Gazos Creek for approximately two-thirds of a mile with points of interest that include two waterfalls, a cathedral-like redwood flat and spectacular views of the canyon.

Bean Hollow State Beach
3 miles south of Pescadero on Highway 1

Bean Hollow State Beach consists of two sandy coves separated by a rocky outcrop. Surf fishing, kite flying, picnicking and beachcombing are popular activities at this beach. There are tide pools to explore with sea anemones, crab, sea urchins and other marine inhabitants. There's also has a self-guided nature trail. This is a good place to stop during winter storm wave surges. The parking lot, perched just above the beach, offers a good vantage point for the watching large waves crash on the surrounding rocks. Swimming is dangerous because of cold water, rip currents and heavy surf. The weather can be changeable; layered clothing is recommended. Facilities at the beach include picnic tables and restrooms. Just across Hwy 1 is Lake Lucerne, an important freshwater lake for overwintering ducks.

Pescadero Parks & Preserves

Memorial Park
9500 Pescadero Creek Road, Loma Mar
(650) 879-0238

Memorial Park is a 499-acre county park located eight miles east of Pescadero on Pescadero Creek Road. The park is connected to Pescadero Creek County Park by a small green belt. The county purchased most of the land for the park by 1924 and commemorated it to the men of San Mateo County who died in World War I. The existing facilities were built during the Great Depression of 1929 when the park then became a camp for the Work Projects Administration. Inside the park there are magnificent old-growth redwood groves, picnic facilities, campground, Visitor Center, Park Store and campfire programs. Pescadero Creek runs through the park, providing a small swimming area. Memorial Park is a popular family camping destination, though no dogs are permitted anywhere in the park.

Butano State Park

1500 Cloverdale Road
(650) 879-2040

Butano State Park (pronounced BYUT-no, meaning "a friendly meeting place" in Native American) is located in a secluded redwood canyon in the Half Moon Bay Mountains, five miles south of Pescadero on Cloverdale Road, or east of Highway 1 off Gazos Creek Road. There are about 3,500-acres of magnificent old redwood groves with miles of dirt fire roads for hiking, offering great views of the Pacific Ocean and the Año Nuevo Islands. Campground facilities include 21 drive-in and 18 walk-in campsites. Restrooms with running water are provided, and drinking water is available at the park in both the campground and day use areas. There are no showers. During the summer months guided nature walks and weekend campfire programs are offered. The weather can be changeable, so layered clothing is recommended.

Pescadero Marsh Natural Preserve
Intersection of Pescadero Creek Road and Highway 1

The Pescadero Marsh Natural Preserve is the largest marsh on the coast between San Francisco and Monterey. Spread out over 500 acres, it was formed about 6,500 years ago. The Ohlone Indians were the first to inhabit the area around the marsh. When the first Spanish explorers came to the area in 1774, trout and salmon swam abundantly in the streams, and wolves and grizzly bears stalked the forests on the surrounding hills. In the early 1990s local farmers built levees and dammed up much of the marsh to expand their agricultural land. After World War II a portion of the marsh was used as a hunting club where migrating birds were the primary targets, as were Asian pheasants raised specifically for the sport. In the 1960s the Sequoia Audubon Society purchased a section of the area, and soon after the state of California acquired most of the original marsh area.

Today the Marsh is managed by the State Department of Parks and Recreation and is a feeding and nesting place for more than 150 species of birds, including the blue heron. It is also a refuge for animals such as kites, deer, raccoons, foxes and skunks. Bird watchers usually find the winter months best for spotting the most birds. During the spring and summer months more than 380 species of plants are found in the marsh area, and there is always a broad spectrum of wildflowers. There is a trail system for exploring the area.

Año Nuevo State Reserve
12 miles south of Pescadero on Highway 1
(800) 444-4445 (reservations)

In 1603 the Spanish explorer, Sebastian Vizcaino, sailed by a rocky windswept point and named it Punta de Año Nuevo (New Year's Point) for the day he sighted it. Today it is the site of the largest mainland breeding colony of northern elephant seals in the world.

During breeding season, from December to March, males battle for mates and females give birth to their young. Most of the adult seals are gone by early March, returning in the

spring and summer months to molt. The weaned pups remain through April. Access to the seals is available year-round through a permit system, but during breeding season only guided walks are permitted; advance reservations are highly recommended.

Año Nuevo Island, across from the mainland, is nine acres of eroding land. The U.S. government purchased it in 1870 and installed a foghorn and lighthouse. In 1904 homes were built for the lightkeepers and their families. When an automated light buoy replaced the lighthouse in 1948, elephant seals and sea lions reclaimed their territory, even moving into the abandoned houses. The island is closed to public access.

MOTHER VOCALIZING TO NEWBORN PUP, WHILE SEAGULLS FIGHT OVER AFTERBIRTH

BULL ELEPHANT SEAL SUNNING HIMSELF

Along Cabrillo Highway

Gazos Grill

5720 Cabrillo Hwy, 9 miles south of Pescadero on Hwy 1
(650) 879-0874 • www.gazosgrill.com

Gazos Grill was started by sisters Claudia Boliba and Stephanie Hare, and has only been open since September 2005, but has already become a homey place for Pescadero locals as well as tourists. The grill features California-style cuisine and offers breakfast, lunch and dinner throughout the day. The soda bar can fix sundaes, banana splits, milk shakes and all kinds of ice cream concoctions.

When the weather is pleasant, there is patio dining; and, if the fog rolls in, it's nice to relax in front of the two fireplaces. On weekends there is live music. Open daily; closed Tuesday.

Pigeon Point Lighthouse
7 miles south of Pescadero on Highway 1

On June 6, 1853 the clipper ship, Carrier Pigeon, carrying cargo from Boston to San Francisco, ran aground near the point. Although the ship was lost, the crew was saved and the area was renamed Pigeon Point. In 1872, after a string of ship-wrecks, Pigeon Point Lighthouse was built with bricks brought around Cape Horn. The light lens was first used in New England, then at Fort Sumter in South Carolina. To protect the lens during the Civil War it was buried in sand.

The 115-foot lighthouse is considered the second tallest lighthouse on the West Coast. Its five-wick lard oil lamp and Fresnel lens is comprised of 1,008 prisms and was first lit at sunset on November 15, 1872. The lens stands 16 feet tall and 6 feet in diameter, weighs 8,000 pounds, and sits in a lantern room that had first been constructed in New York before being shipped around Cape Horn. Although the

original Fresnel lens is no longer in use, the lighthouse is still an active U.S. Coast Guard aid to navigation, using a 24-inch Aero Beacon.

The lighthouse is currently closed to the public, but the grounds remain open. From the boardwalk behind the fog signal building you can watch for gray whales on their annual migration between Baja California and the Bering Sea. Half-hour guided history walks around the lighthouse grounds are available Fridays through Sundays, 10 a.m. to 4 p.m. (No tours on rainy days.)

Pigeon Point Hostel. In 1959 the U.S. Coast Guard built four three-bedroom houses adjacent to the lighthouse. Today these structures offer inexpensive overnight lodging for up to 50 hostellers of all ages, with three male or female bunk rooms. Separate bunk rooms can be reserved for families or couples. Each house includes fully-equipped kitchens and living rooms; guests share bathrooms with hot showers. An outdoor hot tub can be rented in the evenings. For reservations call Hosteling International at (650) 879-0633 or www.norcalhostels.org.

Costanoa Coastal Lodge and Camp

2001 Rossi Road, 10 miles south of Pescadero off Hwy 1
(650) 879-1100 • www.costanoa.com

Costanoa is a 40-acre coastal lodge and camp overlooking stretches of rolling hills. Guests can retreat from the chaos of everyday life, relax in the spa or discover the pace of nature with access to 30,000 acres of hiking/biking trails in four adjacent state parks.

Accommodations include a comfortable lodge with 40 suites, rustic cabins, tent bungalows and even campsites. On the grounds there is a general store, restaurant, private gardens, picnic areas and environmental programs.

Views from Cabrillo Highway

These photos were taken south of Pescadero off Cabrillo Highway. The top photo looks down at the beach below from the Highway. The bottom photo is of the pampas grass along the coast in full bloom along the coast.

Tunitas Beach, Half Moon Bay
7 miles north of Pescadero on Highway 1, at the mouth of Tunitas Creek

Heading north along Highway 1 it's hard miss the dramatic towering cliffs overlooking Tunitas Beach. The beach has a long, colorful history, and was originally inhabited by the Ohlone Indians. When Europeans first started arriving in 1769 with the Portola Expedition, they camped along Tunitas Creek and discovered the Ohlone village. The beach itself is a hard spot to reach, surrounded by private property with "No Trespassing" signs posted, and no parking or other facilities available.

A local legend tells of a sea monster resembling the Loch Ness Monster with a long neck followed by a series of black humps. It was said to live in a cave under the

high cliffs between Tunitas Beach and Martin's Beach, and could be seen sticking its head up "high as the mast of a fishing boat." Today this tale is often interpreted to be a school of porpoises or sea lions playing in the surf.

Gordon's Chute. In 1872 Alexander Gordon, in order to load his agricultural and forest products onto the waiting ships anchored below, built a 45-degree chute off the 100-foot cliffs. Sea captains were unhappy about anchoring in the rolling surf, dangerously close to the steep cliffs and rocks. Also, the chute itself had a major friction problem, tending to burn holes in the produce bags which caused them to burst open when they hit the ship's deck. An 1885 storm finally destroyed the entire poorly conceived contraption. All that is left of the chute today are the eye bolts, which can be seen in the rocks at low tide.

Sunsets along Cabrillo Highway

The California coast is known for its magnificent sunsets. The upper photo was taken during a particularly clear day on Pescadero State Beach. The lower photo was taken along Cabrillo Highway when the pampas grass was in full bloom, touching off some beautiful hues and reflections.

Pescadero Fairs & Festivals

Chamarita Festival

Pescadero, along with other coastal towns, still has residents whose ancestors came to the area in the 1860s from the Azores. The Chamarita Festival (Festival of the Holy Spirit) commemorates the gift of food from Queen Isabella of Portugal, who offered her crown to the church hundreds of years ago in gratitude for the timely arrival of food to the starving people of the Azores.

The Festival is celebrated six weeks after Easter over a long weekend, which includes a Sunday morning parade from the flagpole to St. Anthony's Catholic Church, where the chosen queen leaves her crown on the altar. On their return, the bagpipes play "Amazing Grace" in Duarte's Tavern. At the I.D.E.S. Hall there is a public barbecue and auction, which continues through Monday afternoon.

Pescadero Art and Fun Faire

The Pescadero Art and Fun Faire (PAFF), held on the third weekend in August, is a unique country fair featuring art works by numerous local artists, as well as live music and booths with food, crafts and other items. The hilarious fashion show, where clothes donated to the Pescadero Thrift Shop are modeled, is held on Sunday afternoon, with proceeds going to South Coast Children's Services.

About the Author

I have been a resident of Pescadero since June 2002. My husband and I had originally lived in Penngrove, near Petaluma, for over 22 years, where we raised our two daughters. I had a private practice in Petaluma as a Marriage and Family Therapist and also published a series of six regional bicycling books, which have been in print since 1978.

In 1991 we bought a 47-foot ketch, appropriately named "Adventure," and two years later we sold our home and headed out the Golden Gate Bridge in search of new adventures. We spent ten glorious years living on the sea, meeting new friends and visiting the countries of Mexico, Guatemala, Costa Rica and Panama. After going through the Panama Canal we spent several years on the east coast traveling from Florida to New England.

When our daughters started having families of their own we felt that it was time to return to land. We sold our boat and returned to California living in Pescadero with my daughter and her family as an extended family. A year later I opened a new counseling practice in Half Moon Bay. Because of my love for opera I formed the Pescadero Opera Society, now in its fifth season. We still miss the cruising life so we bought an old motorhome and enjoy land-cruising whenever we get the chance.

After living several years in Pescadero I became an avid photographer, enchanted by the beauty of Pescadero and the coast. I currently sell my photographs as greeting cards and framed photos in local stores in and around Pescadero. Since there seems to be a demand for photographs and information of the coastal area, I decided to write this book.

I love living in Pescadero and consider it my home.

Phyllis L. Neumann

Aerial Map of Downtown Pescadero